DUBAI AND ABU

Travel Guide 2023

A Cultural and Entertainment
Trip in 2023

Patricia Scott

1 *Dubai and Abu Dhabi Travel Guide*

Table Of Contents

Introduction

Dubai and Abu Dhabi are the two most well-liked tourism destinations in the globe and in the United Arab Emirates (UAE). Tall structures, five-star hotels, breathtaking beaches, and a variety of cultural influences can be found in these two cities.

Recently, they have developed into significant financial and commercial centres, luring millions of tourists and travellers from across the globe.

We want to provide you a complete and informative picture of these two fascinating locations with the aid of our travel guide. It will help you plan your trip, choose the best attractions and activities, and make the most of your time in Dubai and Abu Dhabi.

However, we are aware that travelling is not always an easy and straightforward experience. For this reason, we have included helpful tips and advice on getting about these two cities, being safe, and being aware of local customs and manners.

Dubai City Map

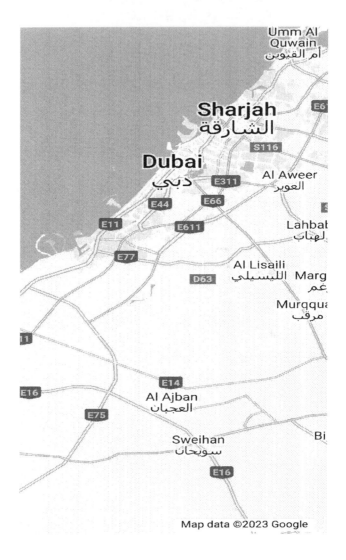

Map data ©2023 Google

5 *Dubai and Abu Dhabi Travel Guide*

Abu Dhabi Map

6 *Dubai and Abu Dhabi Travel Guide*

Chapter One

Geography And History

Due to its stunning landscapes, vibrant culture, and cutting-edge cities, the United Arab Emirates (UAE) is a well-liked tourist destination.

Its two most well-liked tourist destinations, Dubai and Abu Dhabi, are renowned for their spectacular architecture, first-rate attractions, and thrilling nightlife.

If one wishes to fully appreciate the beauty and culture of the UAE, it is essential to comprehend the geography and history of these two towns.

Dubai, the capital of the United Arab Emirates, is a city of contrasts where modernity from the present clashes with traditions and civilizations from the past.

The land was initially inhabited by the Bani Yas tribe in the fourth century BC, starting the long history of the city. During the 1700s and 1800s, the city had a period of growth and development as fishing and the pearl trade brought riches to the region.

When oil was discovered in the city in 1966, it sparked a period of fast expansion and prosperity.

Geographically speaking, Dubai is situated close to the mouth of the Persian Gulf, with the Arabian Desert to the east. The two main areas of the city are divided by Dubai Creek into the Deira neighbourhood and Bur Dubai.

The Dubai Creek, a natural inlet that drains into the ocean and serves as a vital hub for transportation, links the two neighbourhoods.

Abu Dhabi, the largest of the seven emirates, is situated on the Persian Gulf. The city has a rich cultural heritage and a long history of commerce, as seen by its mediaeval souks and markets.

Due to its significant oil reserves and burgeoning tourism industry, Abu Dhabi's economy has grown fast in recent years.

Geographically, Abu Dhabi is an archipelago of islands, the biggest of which is where the city is located.

The city is connected to the mainland by several causeways and bridges, notably the Sheikh Zayed Bridge, which is the longest bridge in the world. A few of the diverse sceneries in the city are the Liwa desert, spotless beaches, and the magnificent Eastern Mangroves.

These two cities in the UAE offer a unique combination of ancient traditions and modern attractions. Dubai and Abu Dhabi won't let you down whether you're looking for a fantastic vacation or a cultural experience.

Chapters Two

The United Arab Emirates: A Brief Overview

The United Arab Emirates (UAE) is getting more and more well-liked among foreign visitors, companies, and students. It is a confederation of seven Middle Eastern emirates, each of which is headed by a separate leader.

Ajman, Dubai, Fujairah, Ras al-Khaimah, Sharjah, and Umm al-Quwain make up the remaining six emirates. The capital and largest city of the seven nations is Abu Dhabi.

More than 80% of the over 9.7 million residents of the UAE are foreigners who have relocated there from other nations.

The UAE is widely renowned for its state-of-the-art infrastructure and energetic cities, but there is much more to this country than first seems.

The region's pre-Islamic civilizations, Islamic history, and contemporary global culture have all had an influence on the UAE's culture, which is a fusion of traditional and modern components.

With this special blending of ingredients, a magnificent community that is renowned for its warmth, openness, and forward-thinking has been created.

A cultural and commercial hub for the Middle East, the UAE has a rapidly growing population and a very diverse economy.

In the UAE, a prominent regional centre for trade, finance, and commerce, several of the biggest financial institutions in the world have their corporate offices.

The UAE attracts many visitors from across the world who come to take advantage of its magnificent beaches, vibrant culture, and hopping cities. The UAE has grown to become a popular travel destination.

Because it is home to some of the most advanced science and technology in the world, the UAE is a powerful centre for innovation and research.

The country is renowned for having cutting-edge energy, healthcare, and educational systems as well as for its commitment to sustainability.

The United Arab Emirates is an intriguing and vibrant country with a unique culture and cutting-edge infrastructure. It is a hub for trade, finance, tourism, and scientific innovation and is home to a diverse population of expats.

The UAE is an interesting place to visit for individuals who are interested in its culture, history, and progressiveness.

Chapter Three

Travel To Dubai

Dubai is a booming city that welcomes millions of tourists each year because of its extensive selection of tourist attractions, luxurious hotel options, and dining and shopping alternatives.

In this book, I'll provide a comprehensive study of each of these three categories.

Tourist Attractions

Tourists may choose from a variety of attractions in Dubai. Anyone with an interest in architecture must see the Burj Khalifa, the world's tallest building.

By taking an elevator to the 124th floor observation deck, one can see the city from a stunning angle. Another well-liked location is the Dubai Mall, one of the largest shopping centres in the world. It contains an aquarium, a theme park within, and a park for virtual reality.

Additionally, the Palm Jumeirah, a man-made island shaped like a palm tree, is a spectacular feat of engineering that gives visitors access to luxurious hotels and resorts.

For those with a passion for history and culture, the Al Fahidi Fort's Dubai Museum is a terrific choice.

The museu tastes something, our brain combines the physical senses with our past knowledge and expectations to produce a unique taste experience.

This phenomenon explains why certain foods may cause strong emotional responses and why different meals may be connected to particular memories or experiences. Getting to know local cuisine might make you more adept at navigating other cultures and chronicles the development of the city, in particular how it went from a little fishing village to a significant global hub for commerce.

The Jumeirah Mosque, one of the few mosques in Dubai that is open to non-Muslims, is another noteworthy location.

For those who are interested in learning more about Islam and its cultural significance, a guided tour is offered.

Shopping and Dining

Dubai is renowned for its top-notch food and shopping options. The aforementioned Dubai Mall is home to more than 1,200 retail locations, including premium stores and high-end designer brands.

The Mall of the Emirates offers a unique shopping experience and has an indoor ski slope and a theatre complex.

Dubai has a broad range of dining options, from sophisticated restaurants to street food. Regional dishes include shawarma, a roasted pork wrap from the Middle East, and matchbooks, a popular rice dish from the Emiratis.

For those looking for a fantastic dining experience, Dubai has a number of Michelin-starred restaurants, including Nathan Outlaw at Al Mahara and Social by Heinz Beck.

Accommodations

Dubai offers a wide selection of lavish housing alternatives, from five-star hotels to serviced apartments. One of Dubai's most well-known hotels is The Burj Al Arab, a sail-shaped building with butler service and privileged beach access.

A less expensive option is to rent a serviced apartment with a spacious living area and a fully working kitchen, like the Arjaan by Rotana.

Even though Dubai has a reputation for grandeur, there are many inexpensive hotel alternatives available, including hostels and guesthouses. The Dubai Youth Hostel in the Al Qusais neighbourhood is a great option for those on a limited budget since it offers affordable dormitory-style lodging.

Dubai is the ideal destination for travellers seeking a diverse and entertaining vacation since it offers a variety of sightseeing attractions, shopping, dining, and top-notch accommodations.

Whether a person is interested in architecture, history, culture, or just relaxing in an elegant setting, Dubai has something to offer everyone.

Chapter Four

Exploring Abu Dhabi

Abu Dhabi is renowned for its deep cultural heritage, elegant architecture, and affluent way of life.

Dubai, the capital of the United Arab Emirates, is home to several tourist destinations, retail stores, and dining options.

In order to give you a complete insight of all Abu Dhabi has to offer, this article will go into depth on each of these aspects of the city.

Abu Dhabi Attractions for Sightseeing
There are many tourist attractions in Abu Dhabi since the city has a rich history and culture. One of the most iconic structures in the city is the Sheikh Zayed Grand Mosque.

One of the largest mosques in the world, it has a stunning blend of classic and modern architecture.

A guided tour of the mosque is available for those who want to understand more about its significance in Islam and its history.

In Abu Dhabi, the Emirates Palace Hotel is another well-known landmark. Beautiful buildings, verdant gardens, and a private beach are all features of this luxurious hotel. Visitors may unwind with a spa treatment or eat at one of the hotel's many eateries.

Anybody interested in history and culture must go to the Qasr Al Hosn Fort. The royal family of Abu Dhabi resided in this mediaeval fort, which is now home to a museum reflecting the history and culture of the city.

Abu Dhabi boasts a variety of parks, museums, and other cultural institutions worth visiting in addition to these well-known locations.

The Abu Dhabi Falcon Hospital offers a unique perspective on the age-old sport of falconry, while the Louvre Abu Dhabi is a famous museum with works of art from all over the world.

A distinctive blend of history, culture, and modern luxury can be found in Abu Dhabi.

Abu Dhabi has plenty to offer everyone, whether they wish to explore the city's well-known attractions, splurge on upscale dining and shopping, or fully immerse themselves in the culture. So why not consider making Abu Dhabi the destination of your next trip to explore?

Chapter Five

Desert Investigation

People have been drawn and enchanted by the desert's beautiful landscape for ages.

From the scorching Saharan sands to the magnificent majesty of the Sonoran, deserts provide an interesting and sometimes challenging area to explore.

In recent years, desert camping and desert safari excursions have grown in popularity as methods to experience the desert.

We will examine the benefits, challenges, and unique experiences that these two approaches to desert travel have to offer in this book.

The Arabian Peninsula and North Africa are two regions where desert safaris are a common way to explore the desert.

These trips often include a guided tour in a four-wheel drive car with a professional driver who is familiar with the local terrain.

The length of the trips might range from a few hours to a whole day or more, depending on the locale and package offered.

One of the main benefits of a desert safari experience is the chance to go to remote areas of the desert that would not otherwise be accessible.

Many safari excursions take visitors to desert regions that are off-limits to the general public, giving them the chance to see exotic wildlife, landscapes, and rock formations.

For those who are unfamiliar with the desert, a guided tour will also provide some safety and security by ensuring that visitors stay on designated paths and stay away from dangerous areas.

Adventures on a desert safari could be difficult despite the benefits. For instance, the hot, dry conditions of the desert may be uncomfortable for anyone who isn't acclimated to them, and the terrain may be challenging to navigate.

Furthermore, if the trip is actively promoted to tourists, some visitors may view the experience to be too commercialised or devoid of genuine.

On the other hand, staying overnight in the desert offers a more authentic and immersive experience.

This kind of activity often requires setting up camp and spending one or more nights in a remote area of the desert.

Depending on the package they choose, visitors may spend the night in a traditional Bedouin tent or under the stars while enjoying basic amenities like a campfire, cooking equipment, and portable toilets.

Enjoying the calm and solitude of the desert at night is one of the main benefits of overnight desert camping. Away from the noise and distractions of modern life, visitors may enjoy the peace and beauty of the desert as well as the pristine night sky.

Additionally, camping in the desert could be a fantastic method to disconnect from technology and reconnect with nature, improving one's physical and mental health.

On the other hand, camping in the desert overnight poses significant challenges. For instance, visitors must be ready for the harsh conditions of the desert, which include high temperatures, strong winds, and sometimes lethal wildlife.

Furthermore, camping in a remote desert area may be challenging and requires a certain level of preparedness and self-sufficiency.

Anyone willing to go out into this fascinating and challenging region may experience something unique and valuable by going on safari tours and camping overnight.

Although each kind of experience has benefits and drawbacks, they both provide chances to engage with nature, discover the many ecosystems of the desert, and challenge oneself in novel and exciting ways. By taking into account the factors stated in this article, visitors may choose the kind of desert adventure that best suits their needs and interests and create memories that will last a lifetime.

Chapter Six

Understanding Local Culture

Experiencing the local culture is a rewarding and pleasant aspect of travelling.

It allows tourists to have a greater understanding of the customs, traditions, and way of life of the people living in the place they are visiting.

The two most obvious ways to immerse yourself in a culture are to visit traditional souks and sample local cuisine.

In this book, I will present a thorough and in-depth analysis of these two pastimes, utilising concepts from cognitive and psychological research to explain their appeal.

A traditional souk is a fantastic way to learn about a place's culture. A souk is a traditional marketplace where goods including pottery, textiles, jewellery, and spices are sold.

A souk's congested and bustling atmosphere may be overwhelming with vendors shouting at potential customers and the perfume of exotic spices filling the air.

Many people find souks to be both thrilling and overwhelming as a result of this sensory overload.

According to cognitive studies, the human brain is wired to look for creative and original experiences.

The brain's reward system is the source of the "novelty-seeking" behaviour, which refers to this need for novelty. When we encounter something new, our brain releases the neurotransmitter dopamine, which makes us feel good.

Visits to traditional souks are made more delightful by this approach.

The novelty of the surroundings combined with the sounds, smells, and visual signals creates a unique experience that our brain interprets as satisfying.

Going to traditional souks may also help individuals develop their sense of cultural competence, which is the ability to understand, appreciate, and effectively navigate through diverse cultures.

Tourists may interact with vendors in a souk and see how people do business to get a better knowledge of the ethics, traditions, and manners of the locals.

Using this knowledge might help you avoid cultural faux pas and communicate better with natives, among other things.

Another way to learn about a place's culture is via its cuisine. Since food is central to every culture, learning about a place's culinary history, present, and cultural values is a breeze.

Experimenting with different foods may also be fun since it excites our senses of taste and smell in a way that few other hobbies do.

According to psychological research, taste is more than just a physical sense; our emotions, memories, and expectations all have an affect on it.

When we taste something, our brain combines the physical senses with our past knowledge and expectations to produce a unique taste experience.

This phenomenon explains why certain foods may cause strong emotional responses and why different meals may be connected to particular memories or experiences.

Getting to know local cuisine might make you more adept at navigating other cultures. By learning about the materials, cooking techniques, and food-related traditions used in that community, tourists may get a deeper understanding of the beliefs and practices of that nation.

Given that food is often consumed in a social setting, it may also serve as a tool for fostering interpersonal interactions.

Visiting traditional souks and eating local cuisine are two excellent ways to discover the local culture.

These activities heighten our senses, satiate our brains' need for novelty, and foster cultural sensitivity.

By learning about the values, traditions, and way of life of the culture, tourists may have a deeper understanding of the place they are visiting.

Conclusion

Dubai and Abu Dhabi are two of the United Arab Emirates' most popular tourist destinations. (UAE).

These cities are famous for their state-of-the-art architecture, lavish malls, and pricey way of life. But for a number of reasons, these cities are fascinating and worthwhile seeing.

In this travel guide, we'll talk about our final impressions of Abu Dhabi and Dubai and provide a thorough description of what makes each of these cities unique.

Let's begin by considering the cultural backgrounds of Abu Dhabi and Dubai. Even though these cities are modern and global, they are nonetheless closely connected to Islam.

Examples of this include stunning mosques that can be seen all throughout the cities and traditional souks, or markets where locals barter their handicrafts.

Abu Dhabi and Dubai have made large sums to protect their cultural heritage. For instance, the Dubai Museum in the Al Fahidi Fort gives visitors a peek into the history and culture of the area.

Moving on to the more modern aspects of these cities, it is challenging to overlook their first-rate shopping centres.

Dubai is home to two of the largest and most luxurious shopping malls in the world, the Dubai Mall and the Mall of the Emirates.

In addition to a wide variety of international brands, these malls provide outstanding entertainment options including indoor ski slopes, movie theatres, and even aquariums.

In Dubai and Abu Dhabi, visitors may engage in a wide range of other activities besides shopping. If you're looking for an adrenaline experience, you may go skydiving over the Palm Jumeirah or dune-bashing in the desert.

For a more relaxed experience, there are lovely parks like the Abu Dhabi Corniche and beaches like Dubai's Jumeirah Beach.

In conclusion, the fascinating cities of Dubai and Abu Dhabi provide a unique combination of tradition and modernity.

These cities provide something for everyone, from their fascinating historical backgrounds to their gorgeous shopping districts and exciting activities.

Even if Dubai and Abu Dhabi may undoubtedly face criticism, they are still popular vacation spots that are likely to have an influence on travellers.

Printed in Great Britain
by Amazon